Careers without College

Security Guard

by Jan Goldberg

Consultant:

Greg Endres
Senior Training Technician
Division of Criminal Justice Services
New York State

CAPSTONE BOOKS

an imprint of Capstone Press
Mankato, Minnesota

Capstone Books are published by Capstone Press
151 Good Counsel Drive, P.O. Box 669, Mankato, Minnesota 56002
http://www.capstone-press.com

Library of Congress Cataloging-in-Publication Data
Goldberg, Jan.
  Security guard/by Jan Goldberg.
    p. cm.—(Careers without college)
  Includes bibliographical references and index.
  Summary: Describes the job responsibilities and work environment of security guards
as well as the necessary training, potential salary, and career possibilities for this work.
  ISBN 0-7368-0039-5
  1. Police, Private—Vocational guidance—Juvenile literature. [1. Security guards—
Vocational guidance. 2. Vocational guidance.] I. Title. II. Series: Careers without
college (Mankato, Minn.)
HV8290.G65 1999
363.28'9'02373—dc21   98-7183
                                                                            CIP
                                                                             AC

Editorial Credits

Kimberly J. Graber and Angela Kaelberer, editors; James Franklin, cover designer
  and illustrator; Sheri Gosewisch, photo researcher

Photo Credits

David F. Clobes, 4, 6, 12, 16, 20, 22, 30, 35, 36, 38, 41, 44
International Stock/Scott Thode, cover
Unicorn Stock Photos/Aneal Vohra, 9, 28; Wayne Floyd, 14; Martha McBride, 19;
  Jeff Greenberg, 24, 32
Vivid Images/John Akhtar, 27
William B. Folsom, 11

Table of Contents

Fast Facts

Career Title _____ Security guard

Minimum Educational _____ U.S.: high school diploma preferred
Requirement   Canada: high school diploma preferred

Certification Requirement ____ U.S.: license required in some states
                              Canada: none

Salary Range _____ U.S.: $10,300 to $25,100
(U.S. Bureau of Labor Statistics and
Human Resources Development Canada,   Canada: $14,400 to $50,900
late 1990s figures)   (Canadian dollars)

Job Outlook _____ U.S.: faster than average growth
(U.S. Bureau of Labor Statistics and
Human Resources Development   Canada: fair
Canada, late 1990s projections)

DOT Cluster _____ Service occupations
(Dictionary of Occupational Titles)

DOT Number _____ 372.667-034

GOE Number _____ 04.02.02
(Guide for Occupational Exploration)

NOC _____ 6651
(National Occupational Classification—Canada)

Chapter 1

What Security Guards Do

Security guards protect people and property. They watch certain areas. They report what they see. They may report problems to police, fire departments, or company management.

Guards may work at office buildings, hospitals, banks, or shopping malls. Guards also work at colleges, golf courses, and parks.

Guards make sure people obey government laws and company rules. Guards stop people

Security guards may work at office buildings, hospitals, banks, or shopping malls.

from going into places where people do not belong. Guards make sure no one steals or harms property. They may stop people who are breaking rules or laws. Some guards arrest people who break laws.

On the Job

Many security guards patrol work sites. They walk if the site is small. They patrol large sites in cars or motorized carts or on motor scooters.

Guards sometimes stay in one place as they work. Some stand or sit at desks near building entrances. They watch people come and go. Some guards sit outside to direct people who come and go by car.

Some guards work in rooms with surveillance equipment. Guards use surveillance equipment to watch or listen to people in an area. Surveillance equipment includes cameras or listening devices.

Guards inspect work areas. Guards make sure doors and windows are closed and locked. They

Security guards patrol large sites in motorized carts.

make sure no one except workers stay in a building after working hours. Guards make sure alarms, sprinkler systems, and heaters are working. They look for signs of fire or other problems that would harm property.

Guards report everything that happens while they are on duty. They often write long reports. Guards note unusual visitors or events. They write down the results of their inspections. Some guards use computers to store these facts.

Types of Security Guards

Security guards may have special duties depending on where they work. Some guards prevent people from taking weapons or illegal goods onto planes, boats, or trains. These guards protect people and property at airports, seaports, and railroads.

Some guards work in museums. Guards in museums protect works of art. They also protect museum displays. They make sure no one steals

Security guards often write long reports.

or harms the displays. These guards may answer questions and guide people.

Some guards help control crowds at concerts, parades, and sporting events. They make sure no one harms property or other people. They stop people from going where they should not go.

Some guards drive bulletproof trucks. These trucks carry money and valuable property from one place to another. Guards protect the contents of the trucks.

Some security guards are bodyguards. Bodyguards make sure people are not hurt or kidnapped. Bodyguards may protect the privacy of famous people. Bodyguards stop reporters, photographers, and other people from coming too close.

Some security guards protect government buildings. These buildings may hold weapons or private papers.

Some security guards protect government buildings.

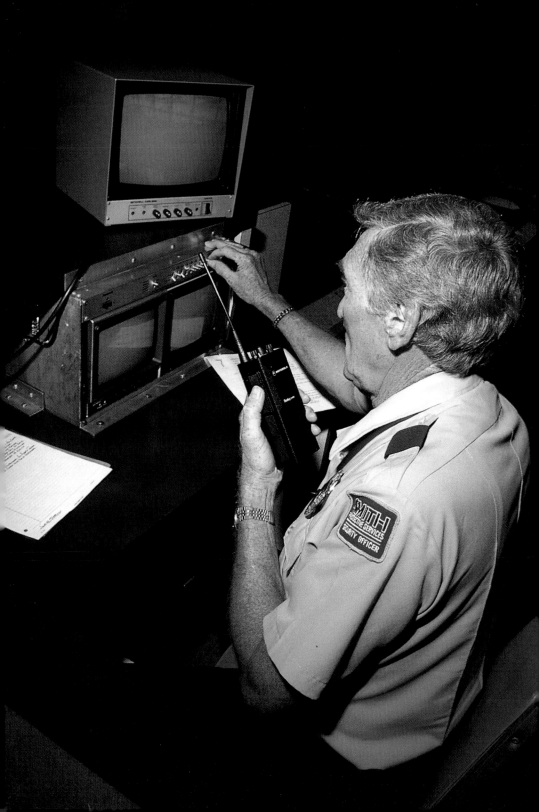

Chapter 2

What the Job Is Like

Security guards can work in-house for companies. In-house guards work directly for businesses. Other guards work for security companies. These companies supply guards to businesses and people. More than half of all guards work for security companies.

Some companies have many guards. Others have few or only one. Guards at small companies often work alone.

More than half of all security guards work for security companies.

Work Environment

Security guards usually work eight-hour shifts. A shift may be during the day or the night. Many guards do not leave their posts for meals. They eat while they work.

Most guards have tasks they must perform every day. One important task is rounds. This is when guards inspect work sites. Guards also make regular reports about their inspections.

Guards must be ready to act quickly in emergencies. Emergencies may happen at any time. They may put people or property in danger. Guards must help people who are hurt. They must stop people who try to damage or steal property. Guards must report these problems immediately to authorities.

Guards always must be aware of risks to themselves. Some large firms use reporting services to help keep guards safe. Guards contact these services several times during each

Many security guards do not leave their posts for meals.

shift. Someone from the service checks on guards who do not call.

Equipment

Security guards wear different clothing for different kinds of jobs. Many guards wear uniforms while they are on duty. Some guards do not want other people to know they are guards. They try to catch people in the act of stealing or destroying property. These guards wear everyday clothing.

Guards carry tools. Many guards carry flashlights, two-way radios, whistles, and special clocks. Guards insert keys located at certain points on their rounds into these clocks. The clocks record the times that guards visit these points.

New electronic wands with computer chips are replacing the clocks. Guards pass the wands over transmitters. These electronic devices are located at certain points on their rounds. The computer chip stores the guard's location and the time. This information can then be downloaded into a computer and stored or printed.

Security guards carry tools.

Some guards carry guns. Most guards do not. Guards must have training and licenses to use guns. Licenses give guards official permission to carry guns.

Personal Qualities

Security guards should have certain qualities. Guards must be able to work independently. They must be able to make quick decisions. They must be able to handle emergencies calmly. Guards also must be observant. They are responsible for finding and reporting unusual happenings. Guards also must be dependable and honest.

Guards must be healthy and fit. Guards must be able to spend many hours on their feet. Their jobs may require them to stand or walk for long periods of time. Guards may have to chase people or run for help. Guards must have good hearing and vision.

Guards should get along well with other people. Some guards have a great deal of contact with the public. They must be neat, friendly, and polite.

Some security guards have a great deal of contact with the public.

Chapter 3

Training

Many security guards receive training on the job. Guards learn to protect themselves, other people, and property. They learn how to deal with the public and how to write reports. Guards also may learn about first aid.

Guards receive training that relates to their assignments. For example, they learn which areas to patrol and which doors to lock. Guards may learn how to use alarm systems. They may learn how to spot and fix problems with these systems.

Many security guards receive training on the job.

Many businesses today use computers and electronic surveillance equipment.

The amount of training guards receive varies with each job. Armed guards receive more training than unarmed guards do. Armed guards train to use the weapons they carry. They learn when and how to use force. Guards who work at dangerous places receive a great deal of training.

Companies usually hire guards who have at least high school diplomas. People can increase their chances of being hired by attending community colleges or universities. Companies often hire people who have taken courses in law or security.

Some guards have studied fields such as sociology or psychology. Sociology is the study of how people live together in different societies. Psychology is the study of the mind, emotions, and human behavior.

Many businesses today use computers and electronic surveillance equipment. A growing number of employers will require guards to have the skills to operate these systems.

Becoming Licensed

Many U.S. states require all security guards to have licenses. Guards in Canada do not need to have licenses. License requirements vary by state. Many states require licensed guards to receive ongoing training. Armed guards usually must complete more requirements for licensing than unarmed guards. Details of particular requirements are available from state licensing departments.

Many states require the same qualifications. Guards usually must be 18 years old. Guards often must pass background checks. Companies check to see that guards have no criminal records. Many states require guards to take classes in certain subjects. These subjects include property rights, emergency services, and law.

Special Employment Requirements

Skill and background requirements vary for different security guard jobs. For example, companies often hire people with military or police experience to be armed guards. These people usually have training in the use of weapons and force.

Some companies require applicants to take special tests. Some tests tell what a guard's

Companies often hire people with military or police experience to be armed security guards.

personality is like. The tests indicate whether the guard is honest and dependable. Many companies require applicants to take drug-screening tests. Drug-screening tests show if people have certain drugs in their bodies. Companies do not hire guards who take illegal drugs.

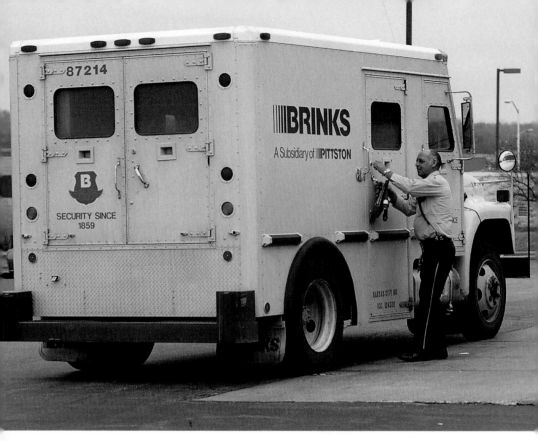

Armored truck drivers must have driver's licenses.

Some jobs require security guards to have driver's licenses. Armored truck drivers and guards who patrol areas by car must have driver's licenses.

People who want guard jobs in the U.S. government must be experienced. They must pass a written test to be certified by the General Services Administration. Most government guards must know how to use guns. The U.S. government often hires guards who have served in the military. Guards for Canada's government must train according to standards set by the Canadian General Standards Board.

What Students Can Do Now

High school students rarely can work as security guards. But they can learn important skills by being school monitors, lifeguards, or safety patrol workers. These experiences teach students how to stay aware of activity around them. The experiences also teach students how to react quickly to emergency situations.

Students who want to be guards should stay healthy and fit. They can take gym classes and join sports teams.

Chapter 4

Salary and Job Outlook

Most full-time security guards in the United States earn from $10,300 to $25,100 per year (all figures late 1990s). Full-time guards in Canada earn an average of about $30,000 per year. The lowest amount Canadian guards earn is about $14,400. The highest amount they earn is about $50,900.

Guards who work for the U.S. government start out with earnings between $15,500 and $17,500 per year. Guards with experience earn an average

Most security guards with experience earn higher salaries.

Security guards check luggage at airports.

salary of $22,900 per year. Guards usually
receive overtime pay for working more than 40
hours per week. Guards receive higher hourly
wages for overtime work. Government guards
also may receive extra pay for working evening
and night shifts.

Job Outlook

The job outlook for security guards is good in the United States. The job field should grow faster than the average for all jobs. The outlook for security guards in Canada is fair. Urban areas in both countries will have the greatest number of jobs.

The number of job openings in the United States is increasing for several reasons. First, there is a growing need for guards because more businesses want protection from crime.

Second, a large number of people are leaving the security guard field. Some leave for jobs that pay more. Others prefer more regular hours.

Third, security companies offer services other people once performed. For example, guards who work for security companies control crowds and check luggage at airports. Guards also protect people in courts. Police officers often performed these duties in the past.

The demand for security guards in Canada also may increase. Canada's government is reducing police forces. Security guards will be in demand to protect people and businesses that police once protected. Most jobs will become available in businesses.

Future Opportunities

Qualified people looking for full-time work will find many opportunities as security guards. Those seeking part-time jobs or second jobs also will find opportunities. People should be able to find night or weekend jobs as security guards.

People can find the most opportunities with security companies. A growing number of businesses are hiring guards from security companies. Businesses hire these guards because it is cheaper and easier than training their own guards.

People who want to be armed guards face competition. Many people want to be armed guards. Armed guards receive higher salaries, more job stability, and more benefits than unarmed guards. A benefit is a payment or service in addition to a salary or wage. Armed guards also have more chances for advancement, training, and responsibility.

People who want to be security guards can find the most opportunities with security companies.

Chapter 5

Where the Job Can Lead

Security guards may advance in several ways. They may advance to jobs within the security field. Guards may earn more pay and more responsibility if they receive more training. They also may advance to jobs in other fields. These jobs may offer more pay and more opportunities.

Advancement within the Security Field

Security guards may advance by moving to large companies. Guards who work for small companies

Security guards may earn more pay and more responsibility if they receive more training.

have few chances to advance. Large companies offer more opportunities and often more money.

Guards also may advance to management jobs within large companies. These guards oversee other guards. This type of job usually requires management skills and some college education. Many large companies use ranking systems. Guards can advance to different ranks as they gain experience and prove their skills.

Some guards advance by starting their own security companies. These guards usually have worked in the field for many years. They often have management experience.

Related Occupations

Many security guards move to other jobs in the protection and security field. They may work as correction officers. Correction officers guard people who have been arrested. They work in jails and police stations. Guards also can

Security guards may advance to management jobs within large companies.

move to jobs as bailiffs. Bailiffs guard people in courtrooms.

Guards may move into related careers. They may become police officers. Police officers earn more money than security guards. Police officers have many opportunities for advancement. Guards may become private investigators. Private investigators gather facts and help solve crimes. Guard experience provides a good background for these jobs.

Security guards can move to jobs as bailiffs.

Words to Know

emergency (i-MUR-juhn-see)—a sudden and dangerous situation

inspect (in-SPEKT)—to look at something carefully; security guards inspect work sites during their rounds.

license (LYE-suhnss)—an official document that gives permission to do something

overtime (OH-vur-time)—working more than 40 hours per week; companies pay higher hourly wages for overtime work.

psychology (sye-KAH-luh-jee)—the study of the mind, emotions, and human behavior

routine (roo-TEEN)—a regular way or pattern of doing tasks

shift (SHIFT)—a set number of hours that a person works

sociology (soh-see-OL-uh-jee)—the study of how people live together in different societies

surveillance equipment (sur-VAY-luhnss i-KWIP-muhnt)—machines used to watch or listen to people in an area

To Learn More

Goldberg, Jan. *Careers for Courageous People and Other Adventurous Types.* VGM Careers for You. Lincolnwood, Ill.: VGM Career Horizons, 1998.

Clinton, Susan. *Correction Officer.* Careers without College. Mankato, Minn.: Capstone High/Low Books, 1998.

Cosgrove, Holli, ed. *Career Discovery Encyclopedia,* vol. 6. Chicago: J. G. Ferguson Publishing, 1997.

Wirths, Claudine G. *Choosing a Career in Law Enforcement.* World of Work. New York: Rosen Publishing Group, 1997.

Useful Addresses

International Foundation for Protection Officers
4200 Meridian
Suite 200
Bellingham, WA 98226

International Foundation for Protection Officers
105-150 Crowfoot Crescent NW
Suite 1015
Calgary, Alberta T3G 3T2
Canada

**National Council of Investigation
and Security Services**
611 Pennsylvania Avenue SE
Suite 2686
Washington, DC 20003-4304

Internet Sites

American Society for Industrial Security
http://www.asisonline.org

Canada Job Futures
http://www.hrdc-drhc.gc.ca/JobFutures/english/
    volume1/665/665.htm

Focus on Security
http://www.kentuckyconnect.com/jobs/s/security/
    moreinfo.html

Occupational Outlook Handbook—Guards
http://stats.bls.gov/oco/ocos159.htm

Index